Violets...

Violets ...

A Collection of Inspirational Poems by

The Women of
ΔΣΘ
Sorority Incorporated

Edited by Shahari G. Moore

Foreword by
Trevy A. McDonald, Ph.D.

 **MP** More Press

Violets: A Collection of Inspirational Poems by the Women of:
ΔΣΘ *Sorority Incorporated*

Compilation and Introduction Copyright by Shahari G. Moore

ISBN # 0-9743394-3-1
LCCN# 2004108092

Cover design by Denise Billups
Photographs by Marcus Fizer

First Printing

More Press
1300 E. 47th Street #353
Chicago, IL 60653

More Press is a subsidiary of More Consulting, Co.

"And she tied a bunch of violets with a tress of her pretty brown hair." She sat in the yellow glow of the lamplight softly humming these words...

Alice Dunbar Nelson

This excerpt was taken from, *Violets and Other Tales* by Alice Dunbar Nelson originally published in 1895. It was bound and re-released in 1988 by Oxford University, Inc. and edited by *Akasha* Gloria T. Hull.

Violets
to Our Founders…

Osceola Macarthy Adams
Marguerite Young Alexander
Winona Cargile Alexander
Ethel Cuff Black
Bertha Pitts Campbell
Zephyr Chisom Carter
Edna Brown Coleman
Jessie McGuire Dent
Frederica Chase Dodd
Myra Davis Hemmings
Olive Jones
Jimmie Bugg Middleton
Pauline Oberdorfer Minor
Vashti Turley Murphy
Naomi Sewell Richardson
Mamie Reddy Rose
Eliza Pearl Shippen
Florence Letcher Toms
Ethel Carr Watson
Wertie Blackwell Weaver
Madree Penn White
Edith Mott Young

Contents

___Spirituality

___Sisterhood

_Love

Includes the Cassie Levy Collection

_Life

Liberation

Acknowledgements

First, I would like to thank God who breathes blessings upon me daily. I am truly awestruck by the way that He uses my life. I will never take our relationship for granted. I would like to thank my mother, Mattie J. Moore, for bringing me into this world. She was the first to expose me to poetry. Even today, she recites her favorite poems. I truly appreciate my mother's support and that of my sister Trizel, my brother Dennis, my niece Justiney, my nephews Walter and Jeffery, and all of my family members. I would like to thank my friends. I am blessed to have too many to name. However, I greatly value Jabir Amarah, Tiffany Austin, Naima Dawson, Gail Upchurch and Ayoka Stewart for their suggestions, support, and critical eyes. I am excited about the energy that each of them bring to the literary world. I would also like to extend my gratitude to professor Sterling Plumpp and Dr. Kelly Norman Ellis, both of whom have changed my approach to writing. Their influence reminds me to never come to the page lightly. I now write with greater depth, meaning, and purpose.

I have been truly blessed by the members of Trinity United Church of Christ in Chicago. As I put the final touches on this document during the Women's Retreat, the energy and power of the sisters refreshed me so that I could complete this project. I would also like to thank the angels at Harris Bank, Kenwood in Chicago. They have supported me as an author, and have empowered me both personally and professionally.

I would like to thank my Sorors for supporting this project. I am truly honored to have the opportunity to work with this collection of poems, and I wish each of my contributors continued success on their individual and collective projects. Special thanks to Soror Trevy McDonald, Linda Everett Moye´, Cassie Levy, Tamara King, and Nicole Lenon. Trevy McDonald inspired me to write during the first Delta Authors on Tour, and she continues to be a motivational force in my life today. I appreciate the level of respect that she commands for independently published authors. I am thankful to Soror Moyé who pioneered an anthology of short stories, thus giving me the courage for this endeavor. I would like to thank Soror Cassie Levy who sent me many poems. She truly possesses a giving spirit, and I am looking forward to her first book of poems. I would also like to thank my running buddy Dr. Tamara C. King. Tamara was the first Soror to contribute a poem to the collection. Her spirit proved to be a catalyst, and soon I was receiving poems from Sorors across the country. I am thankful to Soror Nicole Lenon who took a special interest in the success of this project on a national level.

I would like to thank all of the chapters of our illustrious organization across the globe. In particular the Grand Chapter for granting permission for this project. I would like to thank the Sorors from Theta Zeta Chapter, which is my chapter of initiation and Chicago Alumni Chapter, my current chapter. Last but not least, I would like to thank the lovers and patrons of the arts. Your support keeps us alive! Ten percent of the proceeds from this project will be donated towards Delta National Health Programs, such as Summit V: Health and Healing, which addresses the HIV/AIDS pandemic. To learn more about Delta National Health Programs visit www.deltasigmatheta.org.

Foreword

by Trevy A. McDonald, Ph.D.

The Power of the Shield

The power of the shield
Is what only Sorors can wield
It's more than just sisterhood
It makes being a Delta so good

The shield starts out with trust
Confidence and assurance are a must
Trust is knowing your Soror has your back
She helps you out when you need what you lack

It's designed like that of royalty
Because it's emblazoned with Delta loyalty
Between us deep secrets we share
Loyalty shows we really care

The shield is then painted with love
The perfect gift from God above
The bond of Delta we each hold dear
On your shoulder we can shed a tear

Respect is the shield's first hue
Different opinions are more than a few
While we may not always agree
Your point of view I can still see

The second bright color is support
As Deltas we never fall short
Through encouragement we build esteem
Sorors are always part of our team

Knowledge is the shield's first design
It's intake now, before we went on line
Getting to know each other and Delta was our first goal
More than the mind, but the spirit and soul

Empathy adorns the shield so splendid
When in need it was to me that you tended
You understood all that I felt
And helped me through that with which I dealt

Nurture is the border for this shield
Your care and compassion embraced me as I healed
In Delta nurture helped me develop and grow
It lifts me up when I'm feeling down and low

The handle of the shield is devotion
Its power is more than a notion
To this Sisterhood we are solemnly bound
The power of it is so profound

The power of the shield on which we lean
Is what makes each of us a Delta Queen
It's phenomenal, a great force—full of power
Recognizable by one purple flower

I recently celebrated ten years in Delta with my 41 line sisters of Renaissance 42. Becoming a member of this glorious sisterhood was a six-year desire of mine. This desire started when I was an undergraduate student on a predominantly white campus where Black Greek life among women was non-existent. Most Black women on our campus averted the recruitment efforts by white Sororities seeking diversity. I was always impressed by the five-point programmatic thrust and the insurmountable odds that both our founders and early Sorors faced on college campuses across the nation prior to the Civil Rights Movement. Reading Paula Giddings' *In Search of Sisterhood* enlightened me to the true power of this sisterhood. While I had a few older cousins who journeyed into Delta in the 1960s and 1970s, through reading this poignant text I was introduced to the legacy started by our founders in 1913.

After leaving my Midwestern college campus, I journeyed to North Carolina for graduate school in anticipation of higher learning, professional development, and of course membership in Delta Sigma Theta. I soon learned that membership intake was not in the Chapter's immediate future. A bad economy and a bite from the research bug led me to further graduate study and lengthened my planned stay in North Carolina.

Unknown to me, I was surrounded by Delta women. I learned from these women, worshipped with these women, and lived in communities with these women. I saw them as loyal, devoted, knowledgeable, and nurturing. In 1993 I was asked to supervise the tape ministry staff at my church; however, I was not informed that there was no staff. From the beginning, Emmalene Reade stepped up to assist me. Emmalene, a Delta since 1952, was always there for me when the demands of Ph.D. study took priority. Another Delta, Jane Johnson-Chavis, soon joined the fold and along with the other volunteers, we formed a dream team.

My desire finally had an opportunity to be fulfilled in the spring of 1994 as I was preparing for my comprehensive exams. Careful planning and a very light course load enabled me to make my dreams of becoming a Delta and passing my comps a reality. On April 10, 1994 I was initiated into Delta Sigma Theta Sorority, Inc.

A paper presentation in Australia prevented me from attending the 1994 Delta Sigma Theta convention. It was on the Quantas flight I learned that Deltas are truly everywhere. I met Soror Ella Avery-Smothers who was assigned to the seat beside me on the 14-hour flight from Los Angeles. That was neither an accident, nor a coincidence.

A year later, learning Soror Johnetta B. Cole was the commencement speaker pushed me to complete my dissertation with near lightning speed. I was determined to march across the stage on which she spoke. Two and a half months before graduation a diagnosis of carpel tunnel coupled with hours of tapes in need of transcription made my goal seem impossible. Soror Vickie Newsome was the shoulder I cried on when I considered giving up. Only Vickie did not let me cry long. Soror Newsome was an immense help as she located a transcriber and fed me so that I could concentrate on completing the dissertation.

On that Mother's Day in 1995 when the sky quickly transformed from the beautiful shade of Carolina blue to an ominous and threatening deep gray, Soror Cole didn't simply shake my hand as my Delta Kente stole adorned my robe with Doctor's bars. She grabbed me, hugged me and kissed me, and told me she was so proud of me. That, I will never forget as long as I live.

Sorors have been more than sisters to me. My line sister, Rena Ramsey-Caldwell was the North Carolina "Mom" to me when I couldn't make it home for the holidays. Sorors Patricia Haley and Angela Hare Vereen inspired and encouraged me to step out on faith and start Reyomi Publishing. When I left North Carolina in 1999 to move home and pursue my dream as a literary entrepreneur, I carried with me love and devotion from my Sorors. The continuous hospitality of Soror Lettie Robinson-Goode has made book promotion in the Southeast on a shoe-string budget possible.

Participating in the Author's Pavilion in the 45th National Convention in 2000 was more than a privilege—it was the impetus for Delta Authors on Tour. There I met many Delta Authors, including Soror Stephanie Perry Moore. Ironically, we had a joint book signing in Atlanta that weekend. There Stephanie shared her vision for Delta Authors on Tour with me, and along with Soror Victoria Christopher Murray, DAOT became a reality. Up and coming poets, scholars, best-selling authors and our National Chaplain—the first woman elected Bishop in the A.M.E. Church, have participated in Delta Authors on Tour. Four years, 50 plus authors, and over 20 cities later,

DAOT is continuing to grow by leaps and bounds.

It was at Delta Authors on Tour Chicago that I first met Soror Shahari Moore, who attended a publishing workshop. A therapist by profession, Soror Moore was influenced to revisit her childhood gift of writing. Our paths frequently crossed—at chapter meeting, lectures, and book signings throughout Chicago. Soror Moore's face frequently lit up like a thousand watt bulb as she told me about the children's book she would soon publish. At our September 2003 chapter meeting, she presented *It's Good Sunday,* a story of a little boy who loves to go to church.

I was honored when Soror Moore invited me to write this foreword. I felt even more special when she shared her notebook of early writings from first grade with me during a weekend of book signings. In April 2004, Soror Moore inspired other aspiring writers when she participated in her first Delta Authors on Tour.

Deltas are multifaceted. Deltas are multi-talented. Deltas are all-embracing. Just like the flowers of the African Violet they come in an array of shades reflecting its versatility, *Violets* is sure to display the range of talents and evoke a variety of emotions. Soror Shahari Moore has compiled this collection, which is sure to inspire your spirit, evoke sisterhood, and uplift the life of every reader.

Violets, like Deltas come in many varieties. We are young and old; corporate and military; daughters, mothers, and grandmothers. Across seven regions, which span from Germany to

Okinawa, Deltas shape lives, strengthen communities, and make a difference through public service. Since 1913, public service, the most powerful aspect of our shield, has been the mission of Delta Sigma Theta Sorority, Inc. Soror Moore holds the shields' handle of devotion with *Violets*. Contributing Sorors gave selflessly through this volume. Ten percent of the proceeds from *Violets* will support Delta National Health Programs.

From the classroom to the courtroom, the contributors to *Violets* reflect on their lives, disclose their life's experiences, reveal their deepest emotions, and exhibit courage as they share their thoughts with the world. These Sorors comprise a variety of backgrounds and life paths—both personal and professional. Many are teachers, some are medical doctors, all are extremely talented writers.

Poetry is one of the most personal literary forms of expression. Violets to Soror Moore and to all Sorors whose poems are included in this volume.

Introduction

In Search of Sisterhood by Paula Giddings sealed it for me. I cried as I allowed myself to imagine women who stood strong in the face of racism and women's suffrage in the year 1913. I was a seventeen year old freshman at Eastern Illinois University who had an interest in becoming a Delta. As I sat reading, I was overwhelmed by the strength, courage, and vision of the twenty-two founders of the sorority. Before I had finished the book I had numerous examples of women who had the audacity to be different during a time when assimilation was the "battle cry" of the day and "real women" were limited to the "traditional" roles of wife and mother. Through the establishment of what would later come to be my sisterhood, the women of Delta Sigma Theta Sorority, Incorporated re-defined womanhood for me. I along with ten other women had the honor of being selected as candidates for the sorority in the spring of 1993. I came to call these women my "ships", and the great women who I had been reading about became my Sorors. I did not know it then, but I had embarked upon a life defining experience. Suddenly I had over 185,000 new sisters to embrace.

Since the seminal work of Soror Paula Giddings, I have been inspired by the individual and collective works of my sorority sisters. My experience in Delta has been one that I am proud of, and it is a legacy that I hope to share with my unborn daughters in the future. Delta constantly challenges me and my Sorors to ascend to a higher level in each area of our lives. It motivates us to live, love, and learn with greater depth and passion. It causes us to put every ounce of ourselves into projects which liberate our families, our communities, this country, and our world.

Today, our sorority overflows with over 250,000 members. It is without a doubt the largest Historically Black sorority in the world.

Violets is a collection of inspirational poems by Delta women from various chapters across the globe. The poems that you will read are meant to educate, enlighten, and inspire you— our beloved reader. The poems contained in the volume fall within five basic content areas; Spirituality, Sisterhood, Love, Life, and Liberation. The poets, all Delta women bring color, complexity, and inspiration to the page.

The common thread amongst the 22 contributing poets is that they are all members of Delta Sigma Theta Sorority, Incorporated. Beyond this there is a great deal of diversity in the style of writing, the subject matter, and the backgrounds of the poets. As I read the biographies of the contributors I was truly impressed and amazed by the unique experiences that each poet offers to this collection.

Spirituality is the foundation of our sisterhood. We never want the world to forget that we are first and foremost a sorority based on Christian principles. Our faith in God has provided encouragement in a foreign land for hundreds of years. The poems in this section serve as an invocation for the rest of the works. In all things that we do we must first give reverence to our Creator.

Sisterhood is the "bond of our youth." It has proven to be a blessing to all who have embraced it. Personally and profession-ally my life has been enhanced by the influence and support of my sorority sisters. While we recognize that sisterhood is not limited to our organization, we do feel that we have mastered "the art." This section is dedicated to the all of the sisters of the world. We are sisters in skin and in spirit. Whether you are a member of an organization or not, this collection will touch your life.

Life is the gift that the Creator has granted to us. Our lives are graced with people that we love and interact with on a daily basis. We are also faced with challenges that make life even more complex. Our life's path is influenced by our ancestors who have passed on. The poems in this section focus on themes that one may experience throughout the life span. The themes here include motherhood, family, nature, community, and living with HIV/AIDS.

Love focuses in on Eros/romantic love. We know that this is not the only type of love by far. However, I chose to make it the focus of this section. I feel that it is important to show the beauty and challenges of love relationships to ourselves and our world. Love in the Black community is often enshrouded. We see so many images of self-hate in the media that it is sickening. The poems in this section are romantic and realistic. This section features seven poems from the Cassie Levy Collection. The poems in this section illustrate the balance between head and heart that we all know so well.

Liberation is the last section of this volume. To me it is the most immediate theme. We have been seeking liberation from the oppression laid upon us by America and the world due to our African ancestry for hundreds of years. The Reparations Movement is one of importance and empowerment. We must rebuild and repair the Black community at all costs. Our struggle for liberation in America began in 1619 with the arrival of 20 African indenturers who had been taken from their homeland and given "Christian" names. Upon observing the talents, skills, and abilities of this group, chattel slavery began to take shape and soon after became an "American Institution." Our fight for liberation is evidenced by survival and resistance to oppression during the Antebellum Period, the Period of Reconstruction, the Civil Rights Movement and the Black Power Movement.

The African Violet is native to the Eastern Coast of Africa. Its origin has been traced to Tanga, a town in Tanzania. It is said to have been brought to the western world by a German colonizer in the late 1920's. It produces beautiful fragrant purple blooms, which are symbolic of royalty. Its deep green foliage mirrors our connection to the earth, fertility, and motherhood. Its temperance to water and sun reflects our balanced nature. Its collective beauty is to be shared with the world. The Mud Cloth that lays a backdrop for the cover of the book represents the many textures of a Delta Woman.

It was our founding Soror Madree Penn White who conceptualized the idea of selecting the African Violet as the official flower of our sorority. She felt that it reflected modesty and that the violet like Africans had graced the four corners of the earth. The violet is also symbolic of our bond with the brothers of Omega Psi Phi Fraternity, Incorporated. Soror White's vision proved to be a prophetic one. Today, our sisterhood and programs grace the four corners of the earth and span the globe.

Spirituality

*"Lord, make me so uncomfortable
that I will do the very thing I fear."*

Soror Ruby Dee

Jacquelin S. McCord
If — Then - For

If you want to be free
Then you must know the truth
For the truth will set your free

If you want to receive
Then you must give
For it is in giving that you receive

If you want to walk on water
Then you must keep your eyes on Jesus
For Peter sank when he looked down

If you want something
Then you must ask for it
For you have not, because you ask not

If you obey your parents
Then your days will be longer
For the Lord, your God has given them to you

If you pray
Then pray without ceasing
For the prayers of a righteous woman accomplishes
much

If you want to soar with the eagles in the morning
Then you can't wallow with the pigs at night
For the mud will weigh down your wings

If you want forgiveness
Then you must forgive those who wrong you
For only then will your Heavenly Father forgive
you

If you want to get to Canaan
Then you must walk innocently into the desert
without complaining
For only the children were allowed to enter the
Promised Land

If you wait on the Lord
Then you will run and not grow weary
For you will walk and not grow faint

If you want to defeat the enemy
Then you must fast, pray and praise God
For the battle is not yours, it's the Lord's

If God so loved the world
Then He gave His only Son
For whosoever will - Let Her Come!

Shahari G. Moore
Sista

i remember when sista was
a completely different soul

tormented and confused
she didn't count herself as whole

fass-gurl walkin
sista-gurl talkin

not realizin
the devil was stalkin

always a trip
with a stiff upper lip

she'd flip you off in a "N.Y. minute"
whatever type of drama was goin on

best believe
sista was all up in it

in the chaos of her reality
sista began to shout

shaken by her dreams
she simply went out

on a search
for her soul

Sister found God
He alone made her whole

Billye Rhodes

"I Am"

I am interrupting your regularly scheduled program...

I am an Amaretto sweet and sour.

I am the bridegroom of Jesus.

I am a Texas sunset.

I am a product of William and Mary.

I am the protagonist of free speech.

I am the paintbrush against Ernie Barnes' canvas.

I am the feet of Sojourner Truth.

I am the hair spray of Angela Davis.

I am the waves that carry dolphins through oceans.

I am a survivor of unrequited love.

I am the petal of a purple petunia.

I am the cheerleader of the grassroots.

I am the muse of a strong Black warrior.

I am the check that Mike signs over to his mistress.

I am the tear of Betty Shabazz.

I am Cliff and Claire's forgotten child.

I am a statistic.

I am sarcasm's nemesis.

I am a Griot's untold story.

I am the laughter heard from an afterschool playground.

I am the grimace of a racial slur.

I am the forgotten model of DKNY.

I am the "whistle" that blew from Emmitt Till's lips.

I am an ILL poet.

I am the empty belly of an undiscovered artist.

I am the reason the cops come knockin' at Maxwell's Urban Hang Suite.

I am an Egyptian pyramid amongst a crimson sunset and a crème moon.

I am the cardboard that softens the perfect headspin.

I am the glass that stands between prison husbands and struggling wives.

I am the ribbon in Stevie's sky.

I am the praise of a store front church's choir.

I am the touch of Rouge.

I am the main ingredient of the darkness' constellations.

I am the smile behind the frown behind the smile of Bert Williams.

I am the fifteen languages spoken by Paul Robeson.

I am the spook that sits by the door.

I am a philosopher with no PhD.

I am the American that Lady Liberty turns her back to.

I am the dream of Mary McLeod Bethune.

I am the medal of Jesse Owens.
I am brown, not black.
I am the Lawrys of the Earth.
I am jealous of the person I have yet to become.
I am the perfect melody of John Coltrane's saxo-
phone.
I am a child of I AM.

Michelle Collins
Reality Prayer

Checks - bouncing
Rent - late
Cereal - again!
Humph

Cable - interrupted
Car note -late
Phone - payment plan
I'm mad at cha Lawd

3 degrees
NO man
NO house
I'm mad at cha Lawd

Pay tithes
Live right
I think
What am I to do?

Make Me Over
Heal me
Guide me
Comfort me

Intoxicate me
with your presence
cus I don't want to be
Mad at cha Lawd!

Help me to fall in love again
with YOU
PLEASE help me see
the error of my ways

Cus I don't want to stay
mad at cha Lawd
I just wanna
love ya Lawd!

Cassie Levy
For Every Mountain

For every mountain there are troubles high as a hill
We confront problems but pain remains still
Faith and courage must bring us around
Or the problems of life will keep us bound

How do we find freedom hope or love
Sometimes simple things present the beauty of a dove
We must move on because life will not wait
Confront everything head on and master the gate

Destiny we control with all our might
Confronting the unknown brings us great fright
For every mountain He'll help us cross
The Master is still the Master and remains the Boss

His words have endured yet faith must be strong
For every mountain He's climbed He won't lead you
wrong
So look up to the heavens and strength you will find
He will open your heart and the words will be kind

Your life He will change and a smile will remain
For confidence and faith your life must contain
For every mountain meet it head on and stare
You won't know it's only a mountain if you don't
take the DARE!

Cassie Levy
In My Closet

In my closet, I live in a world full of harassment and pain.
A deep dark place, where struggles and hurt still remain.

I once thought my job was a place of profession and safety.
But in my closet, I recall that thought was much too hasty.

At work I turned my head from his cunning smirks and glares.
But in my closet, I hide like an animal trapped in a snare.

In my workplace I dealt with coworker's rejection and concerns.
But in my closet, my own feelings I was wrestling to discern.

Stepping inside the closet, I remove my happy face and cry.
There were no peaceful waters around and I wanted to die.

Why was I chosen to carry out this task, and should I
just move on?
But in my closet, the Master says, "Remember the
glory of dawn."

So I continued to endure the disbelief and cruel words
each day.
But in my closet, I feel sure justice will arrive "come
what may."

There was no drummer boy to toot my horn or sing
my song.
But in my closet anger arose like a clanging cymbal or
noisy gong.

How many victims have suffered this pain and humili-
ation?
But in my closet, I begin to build real strength and
determination.

My mama didn't raise no fool and my fight was for
dignity
But in my closet, I put on the armor and gave up
humility.

I've got one lifeguard for this journey and that's all I
need.
But in my closet, I ride a storm that's gonna take
prayer indeed.

How many more twists and turns will this wild story
take?
Even in my closet the stress and worry, makes me
need a break.

You can't stay in the closet if you want to be set free.
Because in my closet I become the prisoner of you and
me.

Where is the justice and will it truly prevail?
Standing through the storm is what victory will entail.

I came out of the closet all bruised, battered and worn.
I gave the battle to the Master, cause I was tattered and
torn.

Being in the closet may seem like a safe place to hide.
But standing next to the Master is really the best place
to reside.

Dorothy R. Wilson Coleman
Happy Adversity

I thank God for the word ADVERSITY
It does not mean what it once meant to me
It's not trials, temptation, nor distress
Not hardships, tribulations, nor sickness
Not the tragedies and perils everywhere
Not even the germs that permeate the air

ADVERSITY spells OPPORTUNITIES
To receive the WISDOM and POWER
Which God strengthens his children with
On any day and in any hour.

My joy, Satan always tries to steal
But I trust what God said is real
ADVERSITY only comes to make me strong
I take back my joy and prove the devil wrong

Be joyful and free my Christian friend
For on God you can rely until the end
ADVERSITY has no hold on us
When in our Savior we continue to trust

So be happy in any situation
And greet every troubled face you see
With a hearty "God's blessing to thee"
And "HAPPY ADVERSITY"

Dorothy R. Wilson Coleman
Goodness and Mercy

Goodness and Mercy are everywhere.
From God, they refreshingly fill the air.
To offer us all that we need to exist
in a bountiful life of spiritual bliss.

God's Goodness surrounds us,
and will enter right in.
For his Mercy has covered
our every sin.

So wonderful and marvelous
are these twin gifts to man.
With abiding faith
the two go hand in hand.

Mercy endureth forever
for that we are blessed.
Goodness sustains us always
its time is no less.

As Alpha and Omega,
the two will forever be
Both will follow us all
into eternity.

When one cries "Lord, have Mercy,
please take control."
Goodness steps right in
and soothes the sin-sick soul.

Goodness and Mercy—
what comfort they bring.
"To God be the glory,"
his praises I'll sing.

As with David, they will follow me
until the very end.
God desires the same for each of us
so seek him now, my friend.

Jeannine Woods
Angel

A lonely girl sits on a hot wooden porch
with a tear rolling slowly down her check.
Looking back on her life she realizes that she did
not succeed
in reaching her goals.
 Looking down with a knife by her side
she thinks, "Will this will solve all of my problems?"

As the breeze whips through her soft black hair,
she notices an image of a person coming towards
her.
It was a woman with a box in her hands.
The woman gave her the box.
On the lid of the box there was some lettering that
spelled out

LIFE SAVIOR

When she opened the box
she found a big black book that read

BIBLE

When the little girl looked up to thank her
she was gone.
From that point on
she started reading that book.
In the end, that book saved her life.

Jeannine Woods
Knowledge

What is Knowledge?
Knowledge is a gift from God
A gift that is only given if accepted
One that may change your life forever
Cherish this gift
It was only given to you
Hold this gift
As knowledge is power
Keep this gift
None can take it from you
Use this gift
It will take you far
This gift was made from God
Only for you
Now, that's Knowledge

Alicia Callis
Waiting to Dream

Why is it that I don't sleep at night
Is it the scary movies that I see
Or does my own life host my fright

I try so hard to get some rest
But it's very difficult when there's
Problems, worries, and burdens on my chest

Maybe I need a new bed or a softer pillow to ease
my mind
Should I wash my old sheets
Or get a new kind

Why is it that I don't sleep at night
Is my T.V. too loud
Is my light too bright

To have a good night
Should I clear my place
Remove folks from my personal space

"Someone is sleeping
in my bed
messing with my head"

Look at all this time I've busted
Laying awake all night feeling disgusted
The clock is going off.......it's time for me to be the
boss

I've made up my mind
I'm no longer waiting to dream
I've traded my "queen" in for a "King"

Alice R. Butler Collins
Guides

When you go within
Honor the voices of the ancestors
They will teach
They will speak
When you acknowledge them in your life
You will find your greatness
They are guides
Who stand at the door of your
Consciousness
As your heart beats
And the blood runs warm in your veins
Stop
Listen
Talk with your guides
PA-PA GEORGE
MA-MA LANNIE
DADDY WILLIE
MALCOLM X
SOJOURNER TRUTH
REV. MARTIN
Let them guide you
Consider the counsel of your elders
Find your unique path
Enjoy the possibility of fulfillment

Alice R. Butler Collins
My Path

Finding my path in the sky
I move through a plane with white fluffy clouds
encased in a plane
I move through life in a physical body
viewing a world of
spiritual energy
emotions
I see this world
encased
moving
flowing

Linda Everett Moyé
Soul Speak
from the book *Where Spirits Dance*

When my soul speaks it is in quiet moments
when I have time to think about most anything.
My soul speaks and I remember things I have forgotten.
I know things that I have never been told.
I remember things that I could not possibly
have experienced in this lifetime,
but somehow I know.

My soul speaks and I write on command
what it tells me to consider and to remember.
In quiet moments my soul transforms me
from mother, wife, or business executive into a poet—
one who feels through words which
I cannot exactly explain.

As my soul speaks it reveals me to the core sometimes,
and often it takes me back to places and to loves
I have forgotten to remember but are as much
a part of me as my very soul.

This is no illness and there is no cure.
So when my soul speaks I listen and
when you read or hear my words—

you become a part of my ongoing journey
of self-discovery.

Sisterhood

"Sisterhood is an intentional act of faith."

Soror Shahari G. Moore

Michelle Belle-Villa
We Are Sisters
from the book: *Awakenings: A Collection of Bridges*

We are sisters...
It matters not where we have been
Nor the color of our skin
Shades of every variety
Contained within society

We are sisters...
Talented and tantalizing
Mystical and mesmerizing
Cultured and conservative
Powerful and positive

We are sisters...
Latina, Native American, Caucasian
African-American and Asian
An assortment of nationalities
With unique exceptionalities

We are sisters...
Elegant and exceptional
Smart and successful
Charming and courageous
Vibrant and vivacious

We are sisters…
As our amity grows
Our inner beauty overflows
Undivided by color lines
We proudly speak our minds

We are sisters…
Wonderful and witty
Poised and pretty
Intelligent and innovative
Colorful and creative

We are sisters…
As we lift our voices
And make sensible choices
We have the ability
To improve our community

We are sisters…
Resourceful and resilient
Bold and brilliant
Wise and well-educated
Soulful and sophisticated

We are sisters...
Women of unity
Celebrating diversity
Women of pride
Standing unified!

We are sisters...
Devoted and dynamic
Eager and enthusiastic
Determined and dedicated
Magnificent and motivated

We are sisters...
What determines our sisterhood?
Well, that's not always understood
But it's safe to say
The Creator wouldn't have it any other way

Antoinette V. Franklin
Delta Woman
from in the book *Stories of Sisterhood*

The Delta Woman is like a fresh red rose,
giving beauty wherever she goes.
She has shiny rain drops about her head.
She possess' dignity, sensitivity, and truth.
My sister is a blaze of youth.

The Delta Woman has power and strength.
Her wisdom is never spent.
She is loyal without command,
and kind to those who cannot stand.

The Delta Woman is never vain.
She is stringent in character,
and never ashamed.
My sister patiently waits her turn
to gather praise she has earned.

The Delta Woman is a beacon of light
to those around her and beyond her sight.
My sister is the special one
who dreams, dreams
and gets things done.

Linda Everett Moye´
For Alpha Eta — Fall '73
from the book *Where Spirits Dance*

Red violet pearls and cream
A duck a line a song a dream
Twenty-two one-nine-one-three
Sisters brothers rituals and library

Service worship class "the room"
A book a pin a candle a broom
Stepping reciting learning more
Minerva to watch and not the door

Wisdom virtue compassion and trust
Knowledge membership and love a must
Bonding understanding and commitment supreme
To the red violet pearls and cream

Monique Miles Bruner
In Search of True Sisterhood

I

When I entered college I was unsure
I researched read
and went to all the teas
I looked at the deeds
of all the Black sororities

I was searching from my heart
Waiting on direction from God
My decision was difficult you see
I lifted my eyes from stereotypes
friends and family placed upon me

Then one day I just knew
sisterhood crimson cream and true
The organization that stood for
Scholarship Sisterhood and Service
DELTA SIGMA THETA SORORITY, INC. was for me

II

Senior year at the University of Oklahoma
I went to the rush all alone
Wore my favorite suit
My hair was done
A Coach bag completed the ensemble

I had read – In Search of Sisterhood
And memorized the Delta Founders
I had been to programs presented by Deltas on campus
And given time to community service
I knew all of the chapter members

My GPA was on point
The application burned my anticipating finger tips
I released it to them
I interviewed, paid dues and completed the process too
Eight line sisters later I was a Delta

April 26, 1992 – marked the day
I entered
Delta Sigma Theta Sorority, Inc.
Kappa Alpha Chapter
Committed to Scholarship, Sisterhood and Service...

Emma L.W. Jones
"DELTA" On My Mind

Oh, to be a DELTA
What a wonderful, wonderful thing
I'm on the playground having fun
I guess I'm just a little too young

Oh, to be a DELTA
I don't know where to begin
I've wanted to be a "Delta Girl"
Since, way back when

Oh, to be a DELTA
It's forever in my thoughts
I just became a "Del-Teen"
I'm getting closer to my dream

Oh, to be a DELTA
Those beautiful, positive women
They are the "movers and shakers" you see
The spirit of the community

Oh, to be a DELTA
So graceful, intelligent and proud
I'm really looking forward
To joining that "fine" crowd

Oh, to be a DELTA
I've got my act together
Attitude, grades and money look good
When accepted, I'm a Delta forever

Now, I am a DELTA,
The days of dreaming are "no more"
I'm proudly wearing the "Crimson and Cream"
Making a difference like never before

Tamara C. King
Perilous Journey

A Perilous Journey
It turned out to be
Ten other women
All bonding with me

Long sleepless nights
Never ending days
Determined to be Deltas
Giving God all the praise

This is what we wanted
But were we really sure
Of the challenges and trials
We would have to endure

Just to wear three letters
In Crimson and Cream
Searching for Sisterhood...
What did that really mean

I found the answer in these ships of mine
We laugh
We fight
And still have a good time

In the years ahead
I can only hope to be
Stronger because of them
Because that's what they are to me

Cassie Levy
The Sisterhood Zone

Sometimes it's a card I receive in the mail
An apology for always being late as a snail
Flowers sent when I was really ill
Tasks left undone my role you fulfill

In the Sisterhood Zone you've got my back
Kindness and support when my neck is on the rack
Spirit of a deed no one will ever see
In my heart I know the courtesy is for me

Your comfort and sisterhood bring forth so much
Essence of a jewel giving a gentle touch
"Do unto others" we say is a must
Beauty without courtesy turns to dust

Shahari G. Moore
Two Hundred —Fifty Thousand Strong

250,000 Women Strong
I am one of them

Toiling day and night
Making this corrupt
World right

Born of my mother
Baptized in my Father's Name
They chose me

By this blessing
I am destined
To set brothers and sisters free

Lois Davis

"Watch That Woman in That Red Dress"

When she wears that red dress
She represents the best
Smart Stylish Sassy Lady
Sought after by all
Who watch enthralled

Watch the way she struts her stuff
Onlookers can't seem to get enuf
Poised
Professional
Popular Lady

When she wears that red dress
She can withstand the test
Courageous
Compassionate
Classy Lady

Oh, she's the real deal
You can stamp her with a seal
Spiritual
Sensuous
Sophisticated Lady

When she wears that red dress
You really don't have to guess
No debate here's the update
She reigns supreme
Every girl's dream
When she wears that red dress
She's better than the rest
"She's a Delta Girl"

Lois Davis
Delta Girl

Her dream to wear pearls
with crimson and cream came true.
She is a Delta girl.

She boosts sisters from far and near,
bonds created forever remain dear.
Cherished only by a Delta girl.

She brings unity and
improves lives in her community.
That's what you do as a Delta girl.

She votes, defends, builds, and educates.
Endlessly she works, never seeking any perks.
She is a Delta girl.

Alphas, Kappas, Omegas, independents, and
Sigmas, too,
call her lover, friend; a woman ideal to pursue.
Everybody wants that Delta girl.

Pay attention to the angle of her jaw
held strong and proud, admirers look in awe.
Don't you know she is a Delta girl?

She laughs, dances, loves and inspires.
Effortlessly she motivates, doing whatever it takes.
You can call her a Delta girl.
The best in the entire world!

Margaret L. Whitley
As We Grow Older
A Tribute to all Delta Dears

I look in the mirror and the face I see
Is not the face that once was me—
My hair has changed and steps are quite slow.

My days are numbered, and someday I must go.
But God has been good, His mercy He has shown.
His promise is very true, and in His grace, I have
grown.

I am thankful today, for the long road I've trod—
Not one day could have been endured
Without the mercy and love of God.

Unless one dies in youth, everyone someday gets
old. Please don't ever look down on the aged and
cast them out in the cold.

Instead, treat them lovingly and hope with all your
soul. That God will bless your life so you too will
live to get old.

Love

"I leave you love. Love builds…"

Soror Mary McLeod Bethune

Michelle Collins
YOU... fill my empty room

YOU...

new
>   future minded
>   good-man
>   hard-working
>   devoted
>   purposeful
>   visionary
>   great black bird,

your wings span an ocean...

sexy soldier
>   brother of my soul
>   my king
>   keeper of my heart
>   I do declare

you are my Secret Love

Shahari G. Moore
Trilogy of the 1

I.

I remember
You and Me
Do you?
Twenty years in retrospect.
I turn my mind back.
Grade school anticipation of the first move
6th grade, I like you.
Do you like me too? circle yes/no
The plump and playful messengers J.D. and B.W.
Said you would talk to me tomorrow.
I waited by the Good Humor ice cream truck
With sticky Strawberry Shortcake fingers
He shaped me forever, said I was pretty.
Said I was pretty
He said I was pretty!
Invited me to watch videos
Asked me by the concrete courtside over and over
Amidst the taunting and teasing of schoolmates
Who spewed venomous statements toward the
Budding new girl from the ghetto
With flashy clothes and full lips
How'd she get in?
Questions shaped by
Pompous

Middle-striving
Upper-class
Adults and their offspring
Not you, cause your father knew best, or so I think.
You my childhood, You my friend, My closeness,
My intimacy

II.

Never a label
Simplecomplex introductions
This is Shahari
We grew, we grew, we grew
And pride became our new peer
Both guilty, both guilty, Guilty both of us
Sentenced to a life of looking not leaping
Wondering with closed lips and sly slanted eyes
Talking about and not directly to each other
Double standards and ambiguous emotions
Flood interactions
We reach out with cut off hands
Step out with hobbled feet
Quadraplegics need help too
No evil intent. No pun intended.
Love at the core

Felt in radiant warmth and socially safe kisses
Poured over Amy's chicken sausages, pancakes,
3 a.m's, and sweet souled Baltimoreans
Unexpressed anger cages the heart, hardens you,
hardens me
My presence you question?
I defend!
I was there!
I was there, way back when you wanted me to be

III.

I am confused
But I know what to do
Faithfully I pray
I pray
I pray
I pray to Him for him!
I can't end this poem
I can't end this poem
I can't end it!
You are the 1

Shahari G. Moore
Last Stand in Bronzeville

She stood panting drenched in anticipation
Today, today Lord, something would be said
He had to give in or she would give up trying and
fighting for love

She inhaled balance
Released prayers from sighing tear salted lips
She needed to know now

Squarely in the mirror she noticed a silver strand
Time and justice had met
Soon they would part

20 years of sharing laughing hoping dreaming
Loped off at the peaking point
Sabotaged by fear

"Shake it off" her alter ego cried
Prepare for battle
Gather composure

War paint graced lips cheeks eyes
Powdered full breasts tight buttocks
Caped, she switched out into the midnight hawk to
confront him

and re-capture his heart

Shahari G. Moore
Room

Plant heavy burdened feet
Deep down in fertile ground...
I'm open
New energy and ideas are welcome here

He's gone
Left my eyes lowered
Arms reaching
Tears flowing

He knew
A good woman wouldn't feast alone for long
Birthdays and special times missed
Overlooked and underappreciated

He opened this space for you
So Come...to the table
Bearing new energy love laced dreams
Joy inspiration peace

There's room
Plant your feet root deep down in fertile ground
Gather strength
Sprout tall grow leaves

Alicia Callis
Mutual

We both decided to live apart
But who's in charge of telling my heart

It bleeds in crippled pain all day long
Trying to figure out what went wrong

Although this didn't go according to plan
I still respect you as a man

We both decided to live apart
But who's in charge of telling my heart

Jené Mitchell
Indulgence

Ever since I met you
dreams of a house and kids
have pulled up in the rear view mirror of my mind.
I wanted to FEEL... close to you,
however the feelings where not mutual,
so I chose to be close to you instead, and I
befriended you.
All the while tempting thoughts of consummation
and Firsts
were sitting in my subconscious, shaded in black
First kiss...
First love...
First...
So I kept up my masquerade with a gleeful smile to
hide my love,
and a caring hug to hide my inhibitions.
I was there for you when she did you wrong,
and I bit my lip while listening to you tell me how
she did you right.

And it hurt,
but I settled with the thought that if I was not the
one for you,
I could at least help you find the one.

All the while holding out hope that I was the #2
in your equation of love.

And then it happened,
You came to me deep eyed, sparkling smile,
all the right words, mannerisms, and caresses to
make me fall
in love with you even more than I already was.
Everything you said was right, and I would have
proudly boar your child if it meant that I could
taste the emotions that only you gave, for all of
eternity.
And you indulged me,
I ate from your tree of knowledge,
filling my belly with sugar coated lies, and
chocolate covered fantasies. With stomach full I
exploded over exposing my heart.
Trying so hard to believe that we
were more than just me, in a dream state.

And it ended.
I was devastated, it was over but that was
irrelevant.
The fact that I cared more for you

than you did for me ruined my curiosity.
I no longer wondered what love was like
I knew...
Love was vindictive, and cold
like a bully making fun of your hand-me-downs.

And then you surprised me.
You came back and said those three words,
but I quickly learned that it was not the way I
wanted, needed,
No, No, NO, deserved to be loved.
Yet my naivety and trust still let me be pulled back
into your web.
Still holding that fairy tale of a house and kids in a
picture framed by the glass of my fragile psyche.
And like a poor newborn my soul lies naked in
front of you.
And like a stubborn vagabond it refuses to get
shelter,
and a little help.

And it hurts.
And it happens again, and again, and again.
And you indulge it.

Cassie Levy
A Man and His Woman

"Let a man be a man" is what he said
Is her heart open, or is it dead?
Allow his strength and trust to emerge
Like an eagle in the sky – his powers will surge

Support is what the Black Man seeks
A woman with understanding, a heart so meek
The souls must intertwine to become one
Each task they approach will certainly get done

Joy and pain must cross their path
Real LOVE for each other they must have
Understanding evolves into tenderness in their lives
They become closer like bees in a hive

A woman brings emotions and warms his heart
Their vision realigns – a new journey they start
Compromise is the key as they travel along
Surviving the journey, singing a new song

Their endeavors are inspired true and high
Striving to attain without a great sigh
Relaxation and happiness they must mingle
Feelings for each other begin to tingle

The reward of respect and love they find
Eventually they have a meeting of the minds
They reach a comfort zone and in contentment they
deal
A relationship they enjoy with quenchless zeal

Cassie Levy
Sensual Thoughts

I miss you –
I miss the long conversations that we share.
I miss the expressions from you that show you care.

I miss you –
I miss the warm smile on your face.
I miss the way that you and I embrace.

I miss you –
I miss the way you make me feel inside.
I miss the love within you that you hide.

I miss you –
I miss the touch of your body next to me.
I miss the glow in your eyes I used to see.

I miss you –
I miss the loving man that before me stands.
I miss the soft caress of his loving hands.

I miss you –
I miss the excitement of our romantic trips.
I miss the taste of Godiva chocolate upon my lips.

I miss you, I need you.
You are the TRUE Love of my life.
And I will never, never stop loving you.

Cassie Levy
Late at Night

As I close my eyes and open my ears
Thunder and lightning roll just like tears
Raindrops by the thousands drop through sight
These are the sounds I **HEAR** – Late at night

Long distance brings loneliness to my heart
Many memories I renew as we are far apart
The thoughts fill my mind and seem so bright
These are the memories I **FEEL** – Late at night

A glance at his photo, my eyes move to see
As I smile to remember his face close to me
The warmth of his skin I miss with all my might
These are the feelings I **HAVE** – Late at night

Time will pass and his embrace I will feel
The touch of his skin will tell me it's **REAL**
As joy fills my heart and he holds me tight
The love of my man I **ENJOY** – Late at night

Cassie Levy
Come Closer Now

My heart skips a beat at the sound of your voice.
But seeing you is clearly both our choice.
My mind is so restless with anticipation of you.
Just come closer now.

I look into your eyes and feel my heart on fire.
Is it because we are both filled with the same desire?
Just learn to love me and I you.
Just come closer now.

Anticipation taunts my heart as my soul yearns
With strong feelings inside me that burn
Tired of fighting my heart my darling,
Just come closer now.

The rest of the world won't matter when I see your
face.
Because once we are together we set our own pace.
Can I have your arms around me my dear?
Just come closer now.

I want to dance and sing with my eyes and my heart.

Cause I have always loved you from the very start.
Show me your love my sweet.
Just come closer now.

Love is just a chance for us to take.
We both know emptiness is really at stake.
I don't want that restless feeling anymore.
Just come closer now.

I'll love you now and forever.
And your love for me is just as clever.
Set your soul free to love me.
Just come closer now.

Cassie Levy
"Heart Break Hotel"
A Southern Sista's Revelation

It's about a Sista knowing who she really is inside.
Dealing with a broken heart she continues to hide.

It's a drama she repeats over and over again.
Rejection from tired brothas, who are supposed to
be MEN.

Usually we blame the man for our mistakes.
While the brotha sees your tears and says, "Sista
give me a break!"

You know he's not right, but you continue to go
back for more
The frustration of your heart says "Can't you read
the score?"

He cheats from one sista to another and your self
esteem goes down. The beautiful flower inside of
you withers and turns brown.

Heart Break Hotel you continue to visit
When your mind should say "Is it or isn't it?"

Control your mind my sista and control your heart
With Jesus pay attention from the start.

If he whores from one woman to the next you know
what to do.
It don't take 5, 10, 15 years for you to get the clue.

See, Heart Break Hotel snaps your mind and allows
you to stay.
You get so messed up without salvation, you don't
know night from day.

Take your sense and pride, checkout and grab your
salvation.
Go find Jesus, a new brotha and get a real
REVELATION!

There's a light at the end of the tunnel if you just leave
that brotha.
Get your mind right and you can surely find another!

Be a sista to each other when someone starts to fall.
Give encouragement and love to get her back on the
ball.

Get your faith working with your soul and give
men a rest.
For being right with GOD is truly the test.

You'll walk with a glow and true self esteem.
His love shines on your face like a bright light that
beams.

Heart Break Hotel will keep you off track.
But the Love of the Lord will always get you back!

Cassie Levy
Behind the Mask

If I could turn my head and feel your breath upon
my cheek.
Then I would know that your image really could
speak.

If I turn my head and your smile glared towards my
face.
Then I would know that finally you're in the right
place.

If I could turn my head and your arms wrapped
across my chest.
Then I'd know that your heartbeat would soon lie
upon my breast.

If I could turn my head and read your heart
through your eyes.
Then you'd read mine and know there are no other
guys.

The loneliness really haunts me as I fear you won't
return.
For your love and commitment I continue to yearn.

For years I have loved you day in and day out.
A soul committed beyond a shadow of a doubt.

The sound of your voice sets my soul of love
aflame.
Many times I lamented full of senseless shame.

How do I stop loving you, for I have tried for so
many years?
But most nights I go to bed with a pillow full of
tears.

Many months go by and finally I seal my feelings
far away.
Until I finally see your face again and with you I
wish to lay.

Your love is the part of my soul that I need to feel
whole.
But when you're away it's as if I've buried it like a
mole.

In and out of each other's life we continue to
weave.
But when you're away my heart lingers and grieves.

I want my love for you to shine brightly like the
morning sun.
I want your love for me to be filled with anticipation
and fun.

Many decisions and twists and turns must take
place.
We've reached a fork in the road of this very hectic
race.

Will you go your way without me and I mine?
Neither of us can be the same, it won't be "just fine."

No matter which road you choose it must be your
choice.
Your heart will speak to you, it must be your own
voice.

Your love for me must be free in what ever you
choose.
Interference in your decision would only make me
lose.

Your happiness is important and I want to see you smile.
Your life has struggled with drama, it's been such a trial.

Remember my love for you is truly sincere and pure.
If I could turn my head and hold you, maybe that's the cure.

Cassie Levy
So Real

So Real are the feelings within my heart
I miss him terribly when we're far apart
His expressions of love have become fulfilling
The tenderness of his soul is willing

So Real is his face when I gaze into his eyes
Happiness is an opportunity if we don't let it die
Trusting enough to express how we feel
Compromising a bit becomes the real deal

Forgetting our past, disappointments and sorrows
Looking forward to our day and the promise of
tomorrow

So Real are our thoughts and what we truly want
Letting go of yesterday, otherwise, it will haunt
The road to happiness is not "glitter and gold"
We work together as we shape a new mold

So Real are our feelings, our souls celebrate with
delight
Smiles and laughter emerge each time we reunite

Life

"My Soul is full of concern and love, and I understand the meaning of my own life and the lives of others."

Soror Betty Shabazz

Linda Everett Moyé
Wisdom

Time is not our friend
It has no loyal measure
Live in it wisely

Linda Everett Moyé
To My Children

from the book, *From A Delta's Heart*

Because I am you Mother
I will love you like no other.
One day you will see I'm your best friend,
the best you'll ever have both now and then.
When no one else will understand or care
you will come to me because you know I'll be
there.

It is because you are my special gift from God
you are precious and held in very high regard.
Whatever you grow up to be or do...
never forget that your Mother loves you.

Kimberly Houzz
Transformation

As the world continues to evolve and my body takes on a new design...

a glow if you will/a gift from up above

As I look in the mirror, I'm transforming. This transformation isn't sudden it takes about as long as the upcoming arrival.

During my transformation, I begin to realize that I can no longer just think about me, myself and I.

I transform my mind into new concepts such as:

how/will/can I?

While at the same time developing a loving relationship with my unborn, wondering can I be "everything" I envision in my mind.

Still transforming and building the bond I continue to pray for strength and guidance as my transformation takes a new look;
tears pour, screams fill the room.

I transform…

Then it happens the first cry, the first look, the precious gift that is designed so perfectly as only God could prepare.

He is born...

Alice R. Butler Collins
Son

May You Find Your Path,
Your Way
Your Control
Turn Inward and Search
Heart
Mind
Spirit
Remember There is More Inside Than Out
Peace
Joy
Fulfillment
Fears
Pains
Regrets
Compassion
Transformation
Spend Time In Prayer, Contemplation, Meditation
Turn Inward Consult Your
Spirit Guides
When You Recognize The Voice Of Spirit
When You Understand That Spirit
Teaches
Heals
Reveals

Directs

Empowers

You Will Find Your Ultimate

Control

Strength

Joy

In Surrender

Let The Spirit Take Control

Let It Have Its" Way In Your Life

Give Yourself To Spirit And It Will Never Fail You

Victory is Yours In Spirit!

Alice R. Butler Collins
My Daughter
Lady Baby

The sun rises for me in your smile
You light up my world
Your laughter is infectious
Trust your emotions
Expand your heart

L O V E   M O R E

Invest the energy within and it will bring
you more
Let the spirit guide you
Build your inner sanctuary
Select carefully the things you cherish
You are a lady with the tender heart of
A newborn baby
Treat yourself generously
Let spirit be your guide
My precious lady baby

Cassie Levy
Recognize

Strong as a rock she must take a stand
Who is this woman who raises her hand?
She moves every mountain and climbs every hill.
But who is this woman that never stays still?

She's down in the country and her family she keeps.
The river of pain and problems run deep.
How will she save them as disaster awaits?
But everyone forgot she controls their true fate.

In courage and strength her love stands strong.
The hand of the Master will not guide her wrong.
So many of us know her and wish her well.
But who is this woman, please will you tell?

Don't you know she's my MOTHER, couldn't you see?
With the Love of the Master who else could she be?
I'm grateful for her love each and every day.
Without my mother there isn't much I could say.

She guided my destiny and chances I'd take
With the support of my mother, my life I can make.
I am grateful and dared not to make her cross—
For I love my Mother and she's still the BOSS!

Margaret L. Whitley
"Celebrating Mothers"

It's not always necessary to have given birth
To be part of Motherhood on this earth—
For if in your day–to-day living
You have touched the life of some child
Then you were at that time a Mother
At least for a little while—

Because if in your heart, you really did care
And included children in your daily prayers
And if sometime, somehow, somewhere—
You were needed in some way and
You were there:

Then my sister/my brother
You have indeed been a Mother

Melanie M. Pettway
"What Am I But a Dream?"

I've been love, I've been pain,
Utter despair, confusion, and love once again.

Tried to find solace anywhere,
Comfort, compassion, yet my soul lays bare.

Am I real? Do I exist outside my mind?
Oh, tell me the place to look, and I'll go find
My soul, my heart, the true essence of me.
My passions, my talents, my very dignity!

Do you mock me, as I journey along--
Seeking, being, experiencing-- tell me I'm wrong!

Answer me this, that I may rest,
Has my life been naught but one cruel test?

Am I more than strung together dreams?
Living out a never-ending fantasy, or so it seems.
What am I, but dreams
Yet He is Real

He exists everywhere you'll find
both within and outside our minds.
Anyplace we search we'll see
He is the fulfillment of all our dreams.

Nicole E. Williams
Earth

What is the soul?
Is it something we can feel?
Do we see it in the shadows
That project images of ourselves
On the Earth?

I ask where is the soul?
Can I take it out, fold it up,
Save it from the world and
Its cruelty and only
Bring it out when the
Clouds have parted?

Is it in my hands as I write?
My voice as I speak?
Is it in my lover's touch, hesitant, sweet?

Is it joy, is it love?
Is it the orgasm, brief and tremulous?

I say the soul is
In my hands
My feet
My legs, arms and hair...

Soul is my uterus.

I say the body is the soul and
We being mere mortals on Earth
Can never separate the two…
They are intertwined.

But soul is in the air we breathe in,
Slowly, rapidly.
It is the grass that grows from the Earth.

Soul is the wings of birds
Soul is the wind in my hair
The sun browning my skin

Soul is melanin.

I say these all are one and body is soul
Is mind is spirit is the peace found in
Blackness.

Bodyissoulismindisspiritispeacefoundin
Blackness.

The soul is an electric kiss humming to
The rhythm of infinity.

Soul is you.
Soul is me.

DeReese L. Parram
Constant Companion

You **H**ave invaded my body and become a part of
my existence –
When I wake in the morning my first thoughts are
of you –
Funny isn't it? – You were my final thoughts before
I went to sleep

And the dreams **I** dreamed while I slept
You have changed me – filled the deepest core of me.

Many times I wished for someone to spend my days
and nights with. Someone to always be there for me
– unconditionally
I never dreamed that someone would be you –
Now that I HA**V**E you, How will I survive?

DeReese L. Parram
Constant Companion II.

"How will I survive?"
Those were my thoughts before I closed my eyes last
night
But as I slept I received a new vision that gave me fresh
light

Replaced the darkness & renewed my soul
Touched my spirit and made me whole –
Completed me in a way I never thought possible
To love myself – in spite of myself –was once an obstacle

No longer am I looking for someone or something
To define who I am – It's a brand new feeling
Warmth and joy now fills my body – guides my words
Because my Father, my God – He spoke and I heard

I thank Him for the constant companionship that He has
given me
I will cherish it, honor it, because now I believe
That despite the trials, tribulations, and sickness I
must endure
His love and friendship is everlasting
His grace makes me pure

So despite the physical changes that are sure to
come
My spirit is whole and my turbulence I have been
delivered from
Because He has chosen to be my constant companion
Love and inner peace will be my constant song

Billye Rhodes
Rejuvenation
from the book *Penetrated Soul*

Deep breaths. Deep long passionate breaths. Hold
on to every second that allows you to fill your
lungs way past capacity.
Allow the oxygen to rush through the vessels in
your body.
Open your eyes. Wide. Nah, a little wider. Look
beyond the surface of things.

Can you see every ring of the beautiful oak tree in
the distance? It's been in existence long before you
were even thought of.
Seen hurricanes, survived snow storms, children
who rested against its firm body in the midst of
Hide and Seek games
or carved their names into its wood to prove their
love.

And it's so much stronger than when it started. Its
roots stretch far beyond its foundation. Far from
where we stand. See a creation
greater than yourself. Be humble. Look at yourself.
Don't get the mirror. Use your hands.
Yes. Your hands. Feel.

The distinct arch of your eyebrows, the curve of your smile, the tenderness of your thigh, the toughness of your foot's heel. Only you know where your path has traveled. Run your fingers against your locks, your natural, your extensions, your Dark and Lovely permanent press; the slant of your eyes, the slope of your nose.

And the few pounds you dream of losing. Rejoice in the uniqueness of your physique. No one else can conquer the wondrous feat of duplicating this wonderful creation
His wonderful creation which has been made in His likeness....
Close your eyes. Can you hear that? No. I'm not talking about the ambulance passing by. Nor was I referring to the girls outside jumping double dutch. Are you listening??? Turn down the radio.
Trust me, they will play that song again. Now do you hear it?
Kinda sounds like drums doesn't it? A simple go-go beat.

Move with it. It gets faster. Keep moving. Snap your fingers.
Throw your head back. Smile. Yeah. Embrace this internal rhythm that beats life though to your fingertips, your bones, your soul.
Your heart is not to be taken for granted. Catch your breath. Catch it. Oh, but wait a second.

You smell that? Aside from your too expensive cologne. Smells like yams. Oh Lord, and collard greens with ham hocks! Chile, did you say somebody is cooking a Sunday dinner? Just inhale. Fresh baked dinner rolls with a touch of cinnamon, honey baked ham, rotisserie style turkey.

The butter from the 7Up cake is screamin and you hear it! Freshly squeezed citruses for the lemon meringue pie, homemade banana pudding. You can smell the vanilla extract and frosting made from egg whites and sugar. Fried corn, dressing filled with chunks of pineapple basted chicken breasts.

So right before you explode... taste. Satisfy your palette with home cooking from the heart – nothing

but soul food chile. Evokes warm feeling of home.
Togetherness. Family. Irreplaceable and unmistak-
able. Your foundation; you'll never be able to run
from it. Why would you want to?

Breathe deep.
Exhale.
Laugh,
Sing,
Share...
It's a gift.
Non-refundable,
no guarantees,
no warranties;
just love it.
Live it.
Inhale.
Exhale.
Inhale.
Life.

Willane Charles
Memories of Eleventh Street

Eleventh-was the place to be.
Many new cars and former residents to see.
The three- hundred block is where my memories hold.
Its nickname was "Gunsmoke" after the West of Old.

Eleventh Street was the place to be.

Attractions at McDonald's Grocery where everything's
cheap, the small Southeast Texas town, just north of
Beaumont was a place to keep. For the latest news,
hugs, or a place for old friends to meet. Crowds of
people, sounds of music, and the smell of barbecued
chicken filled the street.

Eleventh Street was the place to be.

Now that the years have passed many lives have gone
their way.
Former residents still drop by during the month of
May. I know that when the last ones are laid to rest,
my memories of good and bad times will stay and my
heart will be the same.

Because,
Eleventh Street was the place to be.

Shahari G. Moore
Streets

cracked chasms
run deep
gathered memories
bubbling over
resting on
muddy waters
turned blue
not sad
just real
they know
red linin
blues jazzin
lips scatin
foot stompin
heels clickin
balls bouncing
double dutchin
tires rollin
spit piss smiles
sunshine
and soulfood
live here
in these
streets

Shahari G. Moore
Total Woman

Inspired by the play *360° of a Woman* by Naima Dawson

As the world turns so does my life
I spin upon my axis, reflecting upon joy, pain,
happiness, and strife
Unsuccessfully the world tried to break my back
Bent me and twisted me
But I did not crack
I look to the skies during my lows and highs
Knowing that I will rise, conquer and fly

I've been the wife, lover, mother and sister all at the
same time
Sometimes your season doesn't have reason or rhyme
Cause life's to be lived and love's to be shared
Fearlessly I stepped out and courageously dared to
Bring passion to the things that please my pallet
All the time knowing in my heart right or wrong
Each lesson is my blessin

Womanist personified, I know who I am
Defining myself, by myself, for myself and no one else
Uplifting my race, pulling as I climb
Bringing sistas, brothas and othas into a higher state
of mind

After my work is done on the seventh day I'll rest
He'll say, "Good Work My Daughter"
And I will have passed His test

Shahari G. Moore
Life

I tasted it upon
breathing
first breaths.
I cling to it with my being.
Light way down
in the pit of my stomach
brings movement to my limbs.
I stride with it,
shake hands with it,
and dance to its rhythm—
fast and slow paces
for designated seasons.
It is colored with highlights
and lows,
textured with old and
new souls,
balanced by
my breathing.
Children play with it,
teenagers flirt with it,
adults confront it.
My life has been kissed
with blessings.
I embrace it.
Life is me.

Liberation

"Because freedom is indivisible, pitting one oppression against another harms us all."

Soror Johnetta B. Cole

Billye Rhodes

Black Is The Funky Color The Rainbow Forgot To Mention

from the book, *Penetrated Soul*

I like to sit on my porch after a light shower
and watch the children run out to the sidewalks
splashing rainbowed water puddles.
The Easter egg yellows
and Molly Ringwald pinks are pretty
but a forgotten beauty
is in the
little curly black haired boys
teasing
the little black girls with
bouncing black ponytails
as they double dutch
their black telephone cords
singing happily
after the rain.

Give me black skin
of Cajun chicken;
Ma Rainey's black bottoms of pots
my momma burned her
collard mustard turnip greens in.
I like Tommy and John's
black feet and

black fists
mascotted by a
sleeeek black panther with
Huey and Bobby
wearin a
baaaaad black beret.
I like the black dirt
that made my
beautiful black man...
in all kinds of shades
and the same black dirt
to grow my ripe red tomatoes.
I'll take that beautiful
black skin that soaks up the suns love
creating beautiful brown hues
without the assistance of lotion or
cancer scares.

I embrace that black face that
Bo Jangled its way into
mainstream America.
I stroke the black that awkwardly sits
between ivory whites

and directed Beethoven into brilliance.
I'll take that shaaaaarp
black three piece suit
on those men
selling bean pies and
Final Calls
in ninety degree weather
on
79th and Stony Island
who politely say,
"Hello sister."

I like to sit on my porch after a light shower
and watch the children run out to the sidewalks
splashing rainbowed water puddles.
The Easter egg yellows
and Molly Ringwald pinks are pretty
but a forgotten beauty
is in the
little curly black haired boys
teasing
the little black girls with
bouncing black ponytails
as they double dutch
their black telephone cords
singing happily
after the rain.

Cassie Levy
Nightmares

Lest We Forget:
Our minds are barricaded –
From a time period we don't understand
We can't imagine the pain
How can we visualize the suffering?

Lest We Forget:
The darkness of the voyage and –
The anguish endured on the ship
Songs of our people crying out for refuge
Chains rattling as shackles connect endlessly.

Lest We Forget:
Years of bondage without hope –
The pain of the generations before us
Old nightmares living in a new world
Creating a place for our ancestors' horrors to rest

Lest We Forget:
Feeling proud of our heritage as we—
Recognize the past to build the future
Dreaming of a world that honors our success
Regretting the transgressions of the
NIGHTMARE before us.

Jenè Mitchell
Rehab for the Human Race

We're addicted to destruction,
jonesin' for a little pain to get us through the day,
injecting the abuse, and rubbing it in on our gums for comfort.
We steal from our souls, promising to give it back, but sell it to
the devil instead.
Just a little hit.
A straight shot to the dome can have us dancing the eternal conga
of slavery.
Yet excuse is the only master we're chained to,
Because we're more of our own enemy than anyone can ever be.
With the green arms of Jealousy holding us down, drowning in a
see of envy.
The times now have me yearning for those school days grandma
used to talk about...
Where they use to shout it out in a church, not shoot it out in
front of one.

I guess I'm speaking to the masses.
I'm tired of sitting on the sidelines while we watch another oppor-
tunity pass us.
We need to learn that togetherness is F-A-B-U-L-O-U-S.

And it's killing me that our people in Africa are dieing of A.I.D.S
And it's happening here too…but not only Acquired Immune
Deficiency Syndrome,
but African-Americans In Dire Straights
But it's us who is holding us back…
We need to work within ourselves to buy businesses not new
Cadillac's

And I find my self using the n-word in passing
seeming to forget that my ancestors died from that harassing.
If we are going to use and abuse this term,
That has hung and raped our forbearers,
Then we need a new definition to make things fairer.

The "New N.I.G.G.E.R" needs to represent a Never Ignorant Gift
of God Epitomizing Righteousness
Not a single mother, a thug, or a crack baby crying S.O.S.

Just remember that rehab is a 12 step program and step number
one is getting over the denial of there being more than one race in
the world.
Cause last I recall Blacks, and Whites, and Hispanics, and Asians
all have the same blood running through their veins.
So I guess I'll start…

Hello My name is Jené and I've been clean for 19 years….and I
call for the rehab of the human race.

Linda Everett Moyé
Simple Acts

To have justice
find a cause
and win the struggle.

To show compassion
find a need
and give all you have.

To see eternity
find a faith
and believe in forever.

To know peace
find the quiet
and close your eyes.

To feel humanity
find a poet
who can touch your heart.

Nicole E. Williams
The Soul's Song

She sang to me
In ancient tones
A song I'd never heard

She sang to me
Naked spirit, deep
From a place I'd never known

She filled my heart
She sang my soul
Went deep and knew my meaning

She brought me out
To sing aloud
My Africa/My Beginning

Shahari G. Moore
Speak Up!

Plastered lips mumbling
Muted incarcerated
words fight for freedom

Shahari G. Moore
The Need

I have to write this.
I have to write right now!
Everything I've held inside
suppressed inside and
relegated to the corners of my mind.
Dismissed, like a lover with no rhythm
and food with no taste.
If I don't talk about it, tell it, say it,
I may die from lack of oxygen.
To live in shame is to live in fear.
To live in fear is to surely die.
I have limited myself too long.
I have suppressed me too often, causing a
slow cancer to gnaw away the life cells
that surround my sweet spirit.
I need release.
So I peel back rocky layers
to get to smooth soft skin.
Through words, I pour living water all over me,
head to toe.

Shahari G. Moore
Personal

personal
place and space
defined by
created for me

uninhibited expression
beware/befulfilled/beblessed
just be

uninterrupted conversation
purging/releasing/flowing

uninhibited by politics/socialtics
all those other ticks/just leeches
sucking out fluid creativity

I cast them aside

Shahari G. Moore
Liberation Song

I will take the hands
of my children
and lead them to
a new way of life.

Teaching them
self love
cultivating creativity
of spirit.

Distant lands
know them
by name
and skin.

This is my dream
my song
our destiny
I long for liberation.

Contributors

Soror Monique Miles Bruner was born in Oklahoma City, Oklahoma. She was initiated into Kappa Alpha Chapter in the spring of 1992. Currently she is active with Oklahoma City Alumnae Chapter. She sits on the Five Point Thrust Committee and the Social Action Committee. She earned her Masters in Human Relations, Masters in Public Administration, and Bachelors in Public Administration from the University of Oklahoma. She is a Professor and an Academic Advisor at Rose State College. She is a member of Prospect Missionary Baptist Church, Phi Kappa Theta Honor Society, the National Academic Advising Association, and the Oklahoma Advising Association. She is a contributor and a co-editor of *Delta Girls Stories* of Sisterhood. She is the author of *Strategies That Empower People for Success in College and Life,* which may be ordered by sending an inquiry to: n2delta@yahoo.com.

Soror Alicia C. Callis was born in Texas City, Texas, and was initiated into La Marque Alumnae Chapter in the spring of 1997. Currently she is active with La Marque Alumnae Chapter where she is a member of the Membership Committee, Ritual and Guild Committee, and the Nominating Committee. She is a member of Fountain of Praise in Houston Texas. She obtained both her Masters degree in Education Administration and her Bachelors degree in Elementary Education/Early Childhood Development from Texas Southern University. Currently she is a teacher at Fort Bend Independent School District in Sugar Land Texas. Her writing is inspired from observations and lived experiences.

Soror Willane McDonald Charles was born in Beaumont Texas. She was initiated into San Antonio Alumnae Chapter in April of 1987. Currently she is a member of Brazosport Area Alumnae Chapter where she is the Sergeant at Arms and serves on the Fundraising Committee, the Founders Day Committee, and the Hospitality Committee. She obtained her B.S. in Home Economics from Prairie View A&M University in Texas. She is a 6th grade Language Arts Teacher at Brazosport ISD. She is a member of the Brazosport Federation of Teachers and the New Hope Missionary Baptist Church. She enjoys reading, swimming, and traveling.

Soror Dorothy R. Wilson Coleman was born in Crawley, Louisiana. She was initiated into Alpha Tau Chapter at Southern University at Baton Rouge Louisiana in the fall of 1955. She currently affiliates with Alexandria Alumnae Chapter. She holds a M.A. in Mass Communications and a B.A. in English/Library Science from Southern University. She is a member of Zion Hill Baptist Church in Pineville, LA. She is a member of NEA, the Louisiana Association of Educators, Cenla Retired Teachers Association, and the Alexandria Chapter of Links, Inc. She is a retired English Teacher and Media Specialist. She is currently working on a book that looks at the history of African Americans in Crawley, Louisiana.

Soror Alice R. Butler Collins was initiated into Lambda Chapter in Chicago in 1965. She is currently affiliated with Chicago Alumni Chapter. She earned her Master of Science in Urban Education from Chicago State University and her Bachelor of

Science in Elementary and Special Education from Chicago Teacher's College. She is certified as a Chicago Public Schools Principal. She also holds a Certificate of Advanced Studies in Administration and Supervision. She is a retired school administrator. During her career with the Chicago Public Schools she served in several different capacities; teacher, administrator, principal, and Liaison to the United States Office of Civil Rights. She also worked as the Illinois Due Process Hearing Officer for the Illinois State Board of Education. She is an author and a Personal Development Workshop Facilitator. She is the Director of Gender Equity for the American Association of University Women. She is a member of Trinity United Church of Christ in Chicago where she is a Teacher at the African Center for Biblical Studies. She is also a member of the Hurston-Hughes Writers Ministry at TUCC. She enjoys videography, photography, yoga and international travel.

Soror Michelle Collins was born in Chicago Illinois. She was initiated into the Joliet Area South Suburban Chapter in 1999. Currently she is a member of Chicago Alumnae Chapter where she is a Pan-Hell Representative and she Co-chairs the Delta Academy. She holds her M.S. in Curriculum and Instruction from Lewis University, a M.S. in Reading from Governors State University and a B.A. in English Education from Governors State University. She is a English Teacher at Hillcrest High School. She is a member of Trinity United Church of Christ in Chicago. She is a member of the South Suburban Chapter of the NAACP.

Soror Lois Davis was born in Bartlett, Texas. She was initiated at the Iota Omega Chapter in the fall of 1974. Currently she is a member of Brazosport Area Alumnae in Clute, Texas. She holds her B.A. in Education with special emphasis in Speech Communication and English. Currently she is a teacher and a debate coach at Brazosport Independent School District. She is a member of the First Missionary Baptist Church in Freeport, Texas. She is a member of the Texas Speech Communication Association, the Texas Forensics League, the National Forensics League, the Martin Luther King Celebration Committee, the Center for the Arts and Sciences Board of Directors and the Vice-President of Cultural Development and she is also a member of and Brazoria County Debutante, Inc.

Soror Kimberly Houzz was born in Chicago Illinois. She was initiated in 1991 at Eta Eta Chapter at Western Illinois University. She is currently active with Chicago Alumnae Chapter where she is a member of the Membership Committee and the Arts & Letters committee. She earned her Bachelor's Degree in Engineering from Western Illinois University. Currently she works as an Engineer for Commonwealth Edison in Chicago. Currently, she is working on a book about a woman who overcomes sexual abuse by a family member, her struggles in life, how she comes to terms with abuse and is able to surpass it to find happiness. She resides in Chicago with her husband Brandon Houzz and her son Kyle.

Soror Antoinette V. Franklin was born in San Antonio, Texas and was initiated into Zeta Upsilon in Chapter in San Antonio Texas in 1975. She is currently active with her chapter of initiation. She serves on the Arts and Letters Committee and the House Committee. She attended Incarnate Word College in San Antonio Texas where she earned her M.A. in Education and her B.A. in Psychology. She also attended Webster University in St. Lois, MO where she obtained her M.A. in Management. Currently she works as an instructor with Lackland Air Force Base where she teaches English as a Second Language and San Antonio Independent School District as a GED instructor. She is a member of the San Antonio Cultural Arts Board, St. Peter Claver Ladies Auxiliary, TEX/TESOL (an English as a second language organization), Gemini Inc, and the San Antonio Poets Association. Her hobbies are reading, watching old movies, and listening to jazz. She is currently working on a book of poems.

Soror Emma L.W. Jones was born in New Orleans, Louisiana. She was initiated into Delta Iota Chapter at Grambling College in 1971. She is a Charter Member of Arlington Alumnae Chapter in Texas where she serves on the Founders Day Committee, the Nominating Committee, the Membership Committee and Delta Academy. She earned her M.Ed. from the University of South Carolina and her B.S. from Grambling State University. She is an educator with the Arlington Independent School District. She is a member of the Cornerstone Baptist Church, where the Reverend Dwight Mckissic is the pastor. She is a member of Phi Delta Kappa, the United Educators Association and the National Alliance of Black School Educators. In her spare time she writes, is heavily involved in community activities, and works with church leadership and youth ministries.

Soror Tamara C. King is a native Chicagoan and was initiated into Alpha Nu Chapter at the University of Illinois on April 23, 1994. She is currently a member of Chicago Alumnae Chapter. She is an Ed.D. candidate of Curriculum and Instruction at Loyola University in Chicago. She expects to receive her degree in December of 2004. She received her M.Ed. in Leadership and Administration from the University of Illinois at Chicago and her B.S. in Elementary Education from Chicago State University. Currently she is a Mathematics Coordinator for Chicago Public Schools. She is an avid stepper, shopper, and traveler. She currently resides in Chicago with her son Armani Gerre´ King.

Soror Cassie Levy was born in Abbeville, Louisiana. She was initiated into Alpha Tau Chapter at Southern University in Baton Rouge Louisiana in 1975. Currently she is a member of Suburban Houston-Ft. Bend Alumnae. She is a member of the Texas State Leadership Team for Delta Sigma Theta Sorority, Inc. She has acted as the State Parliamentarian for the sorority as well as a Membership Intake Trainer, and as a Delta Internal Development Facilitator since 2001. She is a member of the Founder's Day Committee and the Arts and Letters Committee. She is also a member of the Ways and Means Committee and she is the Registration Coordinator for the 9th District of Omega Psi Phi Fraternity. She is the Vice President of Internal Affairs for the World Youth Foundation Board. She is a contributing author to *Delta Girls, Stories of Sisterhood.* She obtained her Bachelor of Arts in Journalism from Southern University at Baton Rouge, Louisiana. She is currently a Management Analyst for the City of Houston's Controller's Office.

Soror Jacquelin S. McCord was born in Meherrin, Virginia. She was initiated into Epsilon Tau Chapter in New York in 1971. She is currently a member of Chicago Alumnae Chapter where she sits on the Membership Services Committee and the Arts and Letters Committee. She is an educator and the CEO of T. Joy Andrea Publishers. She earned her Doctorate in Naprapathy from the National College of Naprapathy. She earned her M.A. at Spertus College in Chicago and her B.S. at Fordham University. She is a member of the Apostolic Church of God in Chicago. She is a member of the National Council for the Social Studies, the Chicago Area School Leadership Council, the Rainbow PUSH Coalition, and the Black Literary Umbrella. She is the author of *A Molehill is A Mountain, Fur Coats in My Closet, Miss America and the Silver Medal,* and *When We Get Straight.* You can learn more about Soror McCord and her works at www.jsmccord.com.

Soror Jené Mitchell was born in Chicago, Illinois. She was initiated into the Theta Epsilon Chapter at Bradley University April 17, 2004. Currently she serves as the Treasurer for Theta Epsilon Chapter. Her major is Molecular Biology-Pre-Med. She is a Facility Supervisor at Bradley University. She is a member of Greater St. John Missionary Baptist Church. She volunteers with Habitat for Humanity and Road Marks (an on campus mentoring group). She enjoys writing poems and short stories, bowling, and gardening.

Soror Linda Everett Moyé was born in Franklin, Virginia. She was initiated into Alpha Eta Chapter at Virginia State University in the fall of 1973. She is currently active with San Antonio Alumnae Chapter and sits on the Arts and Letters and Growing Up Female Committees. She earned her JD from St Mary's University and her B.S. in

Psychology from Virginia State University. She is the Owner and CEO of LEJ Poetic Expressions and she is an Executive Associate with Procorp Associates, Inc. She is a member of St. Paul United Methodist Church in San Antonio. She is a member of the International Society of Poetry and the Texas Leadership Alumnae Association. She is the author of *Where Spirits Dance, From a Delta's Heart, The Courage to Say It,* and *Delta Girls Stories of Sisterhood.* You can read more about Linda Moyé and her works at www.lindamoye.com.

Soror De' Reese L. Parram was born in Chicago, Illinois. She was initiated into Theta Zeta Chapter at Eastern Illinois University in the spring of 1993. She graduated from Eastern Illinois University where she earned her M.S. Ed. in Educational Psychology and a B.A. in English and Pre-Law. She is currently the Youth Development Coordinator at Uhlich Children's Advantage Network. Ms. Parram has dedicated her life to enriching the lives of youth through education and empowerment. She is also the co-owner of 20/20 Visions, a consulting firm. She is the proud mother of a beautiful little girl, NiJa who is six years old. Ms. Parram plans to continue her education, and return to college to obtain her Ph.D. in Education. She loves writing poetry, short stories and plans to write a novel in the near future.

Melanie M. Pettway was born in Nashville Tennessee. She was initiated into Lambda Omega Chapter at Duke University in the spring of 1993. She is currently active with Chicago Alumni Chapter. She serves on the Arts and Letters and Mental Health

Committees. She graduated from Georgetown University Law
Center with her Juris Doctor. She graduated from Duke
University with her Bachelor's in English and Afro-American
Studies. She currently has her own law practice. She is a member
of the Black Women Lawyers Association, the Northwest
Suburban Bar Association and the Illinois State Bar Association.
She is a former editor for CCH, Incorporated and she is the
recipient of numerous awards.

Soror Billye Rhodes was born in Chicago, Illinois. She was initiated into Lambda Chapter in Chicago in the spring of 2003.
She is currently active with her chapter of initiation, where she
serves as the Chapter Historian. She is currently enrolled as a
Fiction Writing major at Columbia College in Chicago, and
plans to pursue her Master's Degree in African American Studies.
She conducts a Poetry/Harlem Renaissance workshop at South
Shore High School of the Arts. She has been an avid writer, pro-
moter, and activist for over fifteen years. Having received honors
for her first short story, *Latent Suspect*, at the age of thirteen, she
continued to soar as a writer. While at Howard University, she
deejayed with WHBC-AM, which afforded her the opportunity to
intern in the Marketing and Promotions Department of V103
radio in Chicago. Ms. Rhodes is a member of Salem Baptist
Church in Chicago. She serves on the Executive Board of
Columbia's African-American writing organization, Black Ink.
She is the author of a collection of poetry entitled, *Penetrated
Soul: some things i had to release,* which can be found at
www.onyxroades.com.

Soror Michelle D. Belle-Villa was born in Harlem, NY. She is a poet, an author, a wife and the mother of two sons. She is a graduate of Virginia Commonwealth University in Richmond, VA, where she earned her B.A. in Education. The former teacher now resides in Virginia and is a member of Mt. Vernon Baptist Church. Michelle was initiated into Eta Tau Chapter in 1980 and is currently active with Williamsburg Alumnae Chapter where she serves on the Finance and Membership committees. Michelle is currently a Certified Water Fitness Instructor and enjoys dancing, singing and writing poetry. Michelle's interpretation of family life, feelings and those around her enhance her poetry. Her stylings are passionate, truthful, spirited and full of life. Most recently she was a contributor to the collaborative project, *How We Got Over: Testimonies of Faith, Hope and Courage.* This charitable endeavor will benefit the children on the continent of Africa orphaned by the AIDS pandemic. The poem, **"We Are Sisters"** is used by permission and appears in her collection entitled, *"Awakenings: A Collection of Bridges."*

Soror Margaret Whitley was born in Chicago Illinois. She was initiated into Alpha Pi at Kentucky State University in Frankfort Kentucky in 1948. She is the former Secretary of the Greater Cleveland Alumni Chapter in Cleveland Ohio, and is currently active with the Courtesy Committee. She is a proud Delta Dear.

She graduated from Kentucky State with a Bachelor's of Science in Commercial Teacher Education. She earned her ADC in Gerontology from Cleveland State University. She is a retired educator. She is a member of the Alpha Kappa Mu Honorary Society and several gerontological organizations. She enjoys writing poetry, line dancing, travel, and scrabble. She is known as the "Poet Laureate" of her chapter.

Soror Nicole E. Williams was born in East Saint Louis, IL. She was initiated into Alpha Nu Chapter at the University of Illinois in 1996. She attended Loyola University in Chicago where she earned a Doctorate of Medicine. She attended University of Illinois where she earned her B.S. in Biochemistry and her B.A. in English Literature. Currently she works as a Resident Obstetrician and Gynecologist at St. Joseph Hospital in Chicago. She is a member of True Light Baptist Church in East St. Louis, IL. She is a Junior Fellow with the American College of Obstetricians and Gynecologists.

Soror Jeanine Woods was born in DeKalb, IL. She was initiated into Theta Zeta Chapter at Eastern, IL University in the spring of 1995. She is a graduate of Eastern Illinois University with a B.A. in African American Studies, and she currently works as an educator. She is currently pursuing her Master's Degree in Education at Dominican University. She is a member of New Faith Baptist Church in Matteson, IL. Jeanine loves animals and looks forward to continuing on the writers path.

Soror Trevy A. McDonald Trevy A. McDonald, Ph.D., is a native Chicagoan and was initiated into the Durham Alumnae Chapter. A current member of the Chicago Alumnae Chapter, she is the Co-Chair of Arts and Letters and the Co-Founder of Delta Authors on Tour. An author, screenwriter, college professor and motivational speaker, she is a graduate of the University of Wisconsin-Oshkosh and the University of North Carolina at Chapel Hill where she earned her Ph.D. in Mass Communication Research. Trevy is the author of the novel, *Time Will Tell* and co-editor of two scholarly anthologies; *Nature of a Sistuh and Building Diverse Communities* and the inspirational collection *How We Got Over: Testimonies of*

Faith, Hope, and Courage. She has also contributed to two devotional Bibles and other anthologies including *Proverbs for the People.* In her work as a motivational speaker she encourages all to cultivate their God given talents and share them with the world. Trevy, a member of the National Association of Black Journalists and the Society of Midland Authors, lives in Chicago where she is the President of Reyomi Enterprises, Inc. To learn more about Trevy McDonald and her works visit her website at www.reyomi.com

About the Editor

Soror Shahari G. Moore was born in Los Angeles California. She is a Diamond Life Member of Delta Sigma Theta Sorority, Inc. and she was initiated into Theta Zeta Chapter at Eastern Illinois University in the spring of 1993. Currently she is a member of Chicago Alumnae Chapter and serves on the Arts and Letters Committee. She is a graduate of Eastern Illinois University, where she received her Masters of Science in Educational Psychology and her Bachelor of Arts in Sociology. She is the CEO of More Press in Chicago. She is also a Licensed Clinical Professional Counselor, and an Assistant Professor in the Department of African-American Studies at Olive-Harvey College in Chicago.

She is the author of *It's Good Sunday*, a children's book about a little boy who loves church. She is a contributor to *Delta Girls Stories of Sisterhood.* She is the creator and co-editor of *The Passion Project.* Shahari made her acting debut in 2003 in *And Then There Was Poetry,* by Naima Dawson. Born in Los Angeles California and raised on the South Side of Chicago, this 30'somethin' Renaissance Woman brings a unique perspective to literature and the arts. To learn more about Shahari G. Moore and her works visit her website at www.shaharimoore.com

Titles by Delta Authors

Chameleon, Ja Adams

Grace Under Fire: The Rhetoric of Watergate and Patriotism, Barbara Jordan Style, Brenda Eatman Aghahowa

Praising in Black and White, Brenda Eatman Aghahowa

Keeping Secrets, Telling Lies, Florence Anthony

Floating, Nicole Bailey-Williams

A Little Piece of Sky, Nicole Bailey-Williams

Maid in the Shade, Jacqueline Turner Banks

Juneteenth: Celebrating Freedom in Texas, Anna Pearl Barnett

All of Me: A Voluptuous Tale, Venise T. Berry

Colored Sugar Water, Venise Berry

The Fifty Most Influential Black Films, Venise Berry (with S. Torriano Berry)

Meditated Messages and African American Culture, Venise Berry (Ed.) (with Carmen Manning Miller)

So Good, Venise Berry

Women's Liberation Jesus Style, Stephanie Bibb

Sky: An Upbeat Black Girls Song, Thema Simone Bryant

Strategies That Empower People for Success in College and Life, Monique Miles Bruner

Shades of Justice, Linda McKeever Bullard

The Intuitive Principal: A Guide to Leadership, Jacqueline Carothers

How to Be: Contemporary Etiquette for African Americans, Harriette Cole

Jumping the Broom: The African-American Wedding Planner, Harriette Cole

Vows: The African-American Couples' Guide to Designing a Sacred Ceremony, Harriette Cole

Pot Likker: Stories for Teachers and Learners, Deborah Peaks Coleman (Ed.) (with Larry Grant Coleman)

Televisions Imageable Influences: The Self-Perceptions of Young African Americans, Camille O. Cosby, Ed.D.

A Wealth of Wisdom: Legendary African American Elders Speak, Camille Cosby, Ed.D. (with Renee Pouissant)

I Want It Now, Na'Kisha Crawford

Glowchild and Other Poems Selected, Ruby Dee

My One Good Nerve: Rhythms, Rhymes, Reasons, Ruby Dee

Purlie Victorious: A Commemorative, Ruby Dee

Tower to Heaven, Ruby Dee

Two Ways to Count to Ten: A Liberian Folktale, Ruby Dee

With Ossie and Ruby: In This Life Together, Ruby Dee (with Ossie Davis)

The Intuitive Principle, Karen M. Dyer

Lanterns: A Memoir of Mentors, Marian Wright Edelman

Tougaloo Blues, Kelly Norman Ellis, Ph.D.

My Rise to the Stars: How a Sharecropper's Daughter Became an Army General, Clara L. Adams Ender

Twilight Moods, Nancy Flowers

The Collection: A Twenty-Volume Collection of Poetry. Rebera Elliot Foston, M.D., M.P.H., M.A.T.S., D.Min.

From These Roots, Aretha Franklin

A Song of Faith and Hope: The Life of Frankie Muse Freeman, Frankie Muse Freeman

In My Place, Charlayne Hunter-Gault

Burning All Illusions: Writings from the Nation on Race 1866-2002, Paula J. Giddings

In Search of Sisterhood, Paula J. Giddings

Regarding Malcolm X: A Reader, Paula J. Giddings

When and Where I Enter: The Impact of Black Women on Race and Sex in America, Paula J. Giddings

A Poetic Equation: Conversations Between Nikki Giovanni and Cotton Candy on a Rainy Day, Nikki Giovanni
Margaret Walker, Nikki Giovanni
Black Judgement, Nikki Giovanni
Blues: New Poems, Nikki Giovanni
Deer in Headlights, Nikki Giovanni
Ego Tripping and Other Poems for Young People, Nikki Giovanni
Gemini, Nikki Giovanni
Genie in the Jar, Nikki Giovanni
Grand Fathers, Nikki Giovanni
Grand Mothers, Nikki Giovanni
Life Through Black Eyes, Nikki Giovanni
Love Poems, Nikki Giovanni
My House, Nikki Giovanni
Nikki Giovanni Poetry Collection, Nikki Giovanni
Prosaic Soul of Nikki of Giovanni, Nikki Giovanni
Quilting the Black-Eyed Pea: Poems and Not Quite Poems, Nikki Giovanni
Racism 101, Nikki Giovanni
Sacred Cows and Other Edibles, Nikki Giovanni
Shimmy, Shimmy, Shimmy Like My Sister Kate: Looking at The Harlem Renaissance Through Poems, Nikki Giovanni
Spin a Soft Black Song, Nikki Giovanni
Sun is So Quiet, Nikki Giovanni
I Am Woman: Walking in God's Divine Purpose, Sha' Givens
Through The Storm, Sha' Givens
Aaron and Gayla's Alphabet Book, Eloise Greenfield
Aaron and Gayla's Counting Book, Eloise Greenfield
African Dream, Eloise Greenfield
Alesia, Eloise Greenfield
Angels: An African-American Treasury, Eloise Greenfield
Big Friend, Little Friend, Eloise Greenfield
Childtimes: A Three Generation Memoir, Eloise Greenfield
Darlene, Eloise Greenfield
Daydreamers, Eloise Greenfield
Easter Parade, Eloise Greenfield
First Pink Light, Eloise Greenfield
For the Love of the Game: Michael Jordan and Me, Eloise Greenfield
Grandmama's Joy, Eloise Greenfield
Grandpa's Face, Eloise Greenfield
Honey, I Love, Eloise Greenfield
How They Got Over: African Americans and the Call of the Sea, Eloise Greenfield
I Can Draw a Weeposaur and Other Dinosaurs, Eloise Greenfield
I Make Music, Eloise Greenfield
In the Land of Words: New and Selected Poems, Eloise Greenfield
Kia Tanisha, Eloise Greenfield
Kia Tanisha Drives Her Car, Eloise Greenfield
Koya Delaney and the Good Girl Blues, Eloise Greenfield
Lisa's Daddy & Daughter Day, Eloise Greenfield
Mary McLeod Bethune, Eloise Greenfield
Me and Neesie, Eloise Greenfield
My Daddy and I, Eloise Greenfield

Violets

Nathaniel Talking, Eloise Greenfield
Night on Neighborhood Street, Eloise Greenfield
On My Horse, Eloise Greenfield
Paul Robeson, Eloise Greenfield
Rosa Parks, Eloise Greenfield
She Come Bringing Me That Little Baby Girl, Eloise Greenfield
Sister, Eloise Greenfield
Sweet Baby Coming, Eloise Greenfield
Talk About a Family, Eloise Greenfield
Under the Sunday Tree, Eloise Greenfield
Water, Water, Eloise Greenfield
William and the Good Old Days, Eloise Greenfield
The Known Stranger, Rachelle Guillory
Grandma's Hands: The Heart and Soul of New Orleans Cooking, Deidre Guion
Blessed Assurance (contributor), Patricia Haley
Blind Faith, Patricia Haley
No Regrets, Patricia Haley
Nobody's Perfect, Patricia Haley
Open Wide the Freedom Gates, Dorothy Height, Ph.D.
A Question of Manhood: A Reader in U.S. Black Men's History and A Shining Thread
of Hope: The History of Black Women in America, Darlene Clark-Hine, Ph.D.
Black Victory: The Rise and Fall of the White Primary in Texas, Darlene Clark Hine, Ph.D.
Black Women in America: A Historical Encyclopedia, Darlene Clark-Hine, Ph.D. (with Elsa Barkley
Brown and Rosalyn Terborg-Penn)
Black Women in White: Racial Conflict and Cooperation in the Nursing Profession, 1890-1950, Darlene
Clark Hine, Ph.D.
Crossing Boundaries: Comparative History of Black People in Diaspora, Darlene Clark- Hine, Ph.D.
(with Jacqueline McLeod-Hine)
Hine Sight: Black Women and the Re-Construction of America History, Darlene Clark Hine, Ph.D.
Masculinity, Darlene Clark-Hine, Ph.D. (with Earnestine Jenkins)
More Than Chattel: Black Women and Slavery in the Americas, Darlene Clark-Hine, Ph.D. (with
David Barry Gaspar)
Speak Truth to Power: Black Professional Class in United States History, Darlene Clark-Hine, Ph.D.
The Harvard Guide to African-American History, Darlene Clark-Hine, Ph.D. (with, William C. Hine
and Stanley Harrold)
"We Specialize in the Wholly Impossible": A Reader in Black Women's History, Darlene Clark Hine,
Ph.D. (with Wilma King and Linda Reed)
Degree of Caution, Sibyl Avery Jackson
Everything Has a Price, Veraunda Jackson, Esq.
You Don't Have to Settle, Veraunda Jackson, Esq.
Beyond Our Mother's Footsteps, Breggie James
Sister Secrets, Breggie James
Principles of P, Annie Tyson Jett
Bebe's By Golly Wow, Yolanda Joe
Details at Ten, Yolanda Joe writing as Ardella Garland
Falling Leaves of Ivy, Yolanda Joe
The Hatwearer's Lesson, Yolanda Joe
He Say, She Say, Yolanda Joe
Hit Time, Yolanda Joe writing as Ardella Garland
My Fine Lady, Yolanda Joe
This Just In, Yolanda Joe
Songs of a Sistermom: Motherhood Poems", Celeste Johnson

Just Gotta Shout: Life Should Make You Shout, Meme Kelly
On Edge, Meme Kelly
Accept No Limitations: A Black Woman Encounters Corporate America, Marjorie L. Kimbrough
Beyond Limitations: Encouragement and Inspiration for the Start of Your Career, Marjorie L. Kimbrough
Coffee Break Devotions, Marjorie L. Kimbrough
Coffee Breaks of Faith, Marjorie L. Kimbrough
Everyday Miracles: Realizing God's Presence in Ordinary Life, Marjorie L. Kimbrough (Ed.)
She is Worthy: Encounters with Biblical Women, Marjorie L. Kimbrough
Stories Between the Testaments: Meeting of the People of the Apocrapha, Marjorie L. Kimbrough
I Can't Cry: A Journey from Shame to Redemption, Traci Marquis
A Molehill is a Mountain, Jacquelin McCord
Fur Coats in My Closet, Jacquelin McCord
Miss America and the Silver Medal, Jacquelin McCord
When We Get Straight, Jacquelin McCord
Building Diverse Communities: Applications of Communication Research, Trevy A. McDonald, Ph.D. (Ed.) (with Mark P. Orbe, Ph.D. and T. Ford-Ahmed, Ph.D.)
How We Got Over: Testimonies of Faith, Hope, and Courage, Trevy A. McDonald, Ph.D. (Ed.) (with Bettye J. Allen, Ed.D.)
Nature of a Sistuh: Black Women's Lived Experiences in Contemporary Culture, Trevy A. McDonald, Ph.D. (Ed.) (with T. Ford-Ahmed, Ph.D.)
Time Will Tell, Trevy A. McDonald, Ph.D.
We Didn't Come Here to Play: How to Win the Publishing Game, Trevy A. McDonald, Ph.D. (with J.L. Woodson, Naleighna Kai, and Soror Avalon Betts-Gaston, Esq.)
FROM GHETTO TO GOD: The Incredible Journey of NFL Star: Reggie Rucker, Nadine McIlwain (with Reggie Rucker)
Journey to the Well, Vashti Murphy McKenzie
Not Without a Struggle, Vashti Murphy McKenzie
Strength in the Struggle, Vashti Murphy McKenzie
The Church Ladies' Celestial Suppers and Sensible Advice, Brenda Rhodes Miller
The Church Ladies' Divine Desserts and Sweet Recollections, Brenda Rhodes Miller
The Laying on of Hands, Brenda Rhodes Miller
Together for Good: Lessons from 55 Years of Marriage, Ella Mitchell (with Henry Mitchell)
It's Good Sunday!, Shahari G. Moore
A Love Like No Otha, Stephanie Perry Moore
Equally Yoked, Stephanie Perry Moore
Finally Sure, Stephanie Perry Moore
Flame, Stephanie Perry Moore
Sober Faith, Stephanie Perry Moore
Staying Pure, Stephanie Perry Moore
Surrendered Heart, Stephanie Perry Moore
Sweetest Gift, Stephanie Perry Moore
Totally Free, Stephanie Perry Moore
Delta Girls: Stories of Sisterhood, Linda Everett Moyè, JD
From a Delta's Heart, Linda Everett Moyè, JD
The Courage to Say It, Linda Everett Moyè, JD
Where Spirits Dance, Linda Everett Moyè, JD
Blessed Assurance, Victoria Christopher Murray
Joy, Victoria Christopher Murray
Temptation, Victoria Christopher Murray
Truth Be Told, Victoria Christopher Murray

The Black House, Kim Ransom
Penetrated Soul, Billye Holiday Rhodes
An Evening of Blackberry Whispers, Angela Ray
Black Men in the Image of God, Dorothy Winbush Riley
Black Women in the Image of God, Dorothy Winbush Riley
The Complete Kwanzaa, Dorothy Winbush Riley
Like a Second Layer of Skin: 100 Affirmations for Faithful Living, Dorothy Winbush Riley
Ties that Bind Way Down Deep, Monique Gilmore-Scott
The Puzzle, Tracie J. Scott
Don't Just Tell Me To Get Over Him!, Karen Arnitria Shaw
The Book of Names, Karen Arnitria Shaw
A Fenced Yard, Penny Harris Smith
Shaded Lives: African-American Women and Television, Beretta E. Smith-Shomade, Ph.D.
Cubicles, Camika Spencer
When All Hell Breaks Loose, Camika Spencer
A Prince In Chains, Crystal Perkins Stell
Never Knew A Father's Love, Crystal Perkins Stell
Soiled Pillowcases, Crystal Perkins Stell
I Know What Love Ain't, D. Zenobia Swift
Just a Little Talk With Jesus, Raykel E. Tolson
Esther, Mary Elizabeth Vroman
Harlem Summer, Mary Elizabeth Vroman
Shaped to Its Purpose, Mary Elizabeth Vroman
The African-American Struggle for Legal Equity in American History, Carole Boston Weatherford
Freedom on the Menu: The Greensboro Sit-Ins, Carole Boston Weatherford Grandma and Me, Carole Boston Weatherford
Great African-American Lawyers: Raising the Bar for Freedom, Carole Boston Weatherford
Jazz Baby, Carole Boston Weatherford
Juneteenth Jamboree, Carole Boston Weatherford
Let Them Play: The Story of the Canon Street YMCA All Stars, Carole Boston Weatherford
Me and the Family Tree, Carole Boston Weatherford
Mighty Menfolk, Carole Boston Weatherford
Princeville: The 500-Year Flood, Carole Boston Weatherford
Remember the Bridge: Poems of a People, Carole Boston Weatherford
Sidewalk Chalk: Poems of the City, Carole Boston Weatherford
Sink or Swim: African-American Lifesavers on the Outer Banks, Carole Boston Weatherford
Somebody's Knocking at Your Door: AIDS and the African-American Church, Carole Boston Weatherford
The Sound that Jazz Makes, Carole Boston Weatherford
Stormy Weather, Carole Boston Weatherford
Tarbaby on the Soapbox, Carole Boston Weatherford
Strangers in the Land of Paradise, Lillian S. Williams
A Fool's Paradise, Nancy Flowers Wilson
The Trouble I See, Vickie L. Wright Wilson
African-American Literature: An Anthology, Demetrice A. Worley, D.A., (Ed.) (with Jesse Perry)
Language and Image in Reading-Writing Classroom: Teaching Vision, Demetrice A. Worley, D.A. (Ed) (Kristie Fleckenstein and Linda Callendrillo)
Reflections on a Gift of Watermelon Pickle . . . And Other Modern Verse, Demetrice A. Worley, D.A. (Ed) (et. al)
Tonic for Your Mind, Delanea Louise Johnson Wyatt